Beagle Barkstrong

A Space Story

By Jamie Boot

For Poppy and Alfie

Barkstrong was also a tough and brave dog, who would grow up to have the most amazing job.

Ahead of his class he had
always been,
he learned to fly planes at
the age of sixteen.

During his studies he was
called up for service,
but being a Navy pilot would
not be his purpose.

In these days, no one had
been to the moon,
President Kennel-dy would
send a dog soon.

Barkstrong jumped
up when he heard
the news,
working for NASA
would be the job
that he'd choose.

Testing fast planes was how it all began,
but Barkstrong dreamt of being a spaceman.

Barkstrong was chosen to
command a mission,
to land on the moon would be
it's main ambition.

He was going to space, no
longer a dream,
Buzz hound and Border Colin
made up his team.

On the day of the launch, the whole world tuned in, "Godspeed spacedogs, let your journey begin!"

The countdown commenced,
the rockets roared,
up into the sky the spacedogs
soared!

Another blast from the rocket took the spaceship higher, mission control rang to make the checks they require.

The flight was going well, they
could see the moon,
ahead of time, they'd be there
soon.

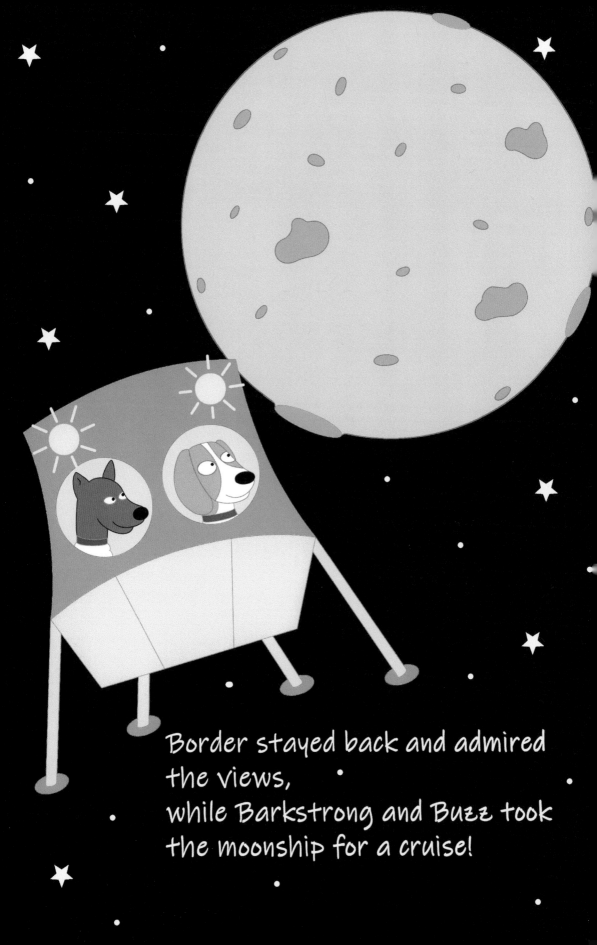

Border stayed back and admired
the views,
while Barkstrong and Buzz took
the moonship for a cruise!

They were coming in too fast,
over shooting the mark,
no problem for Barkstrong,
a walk in the park!

Still chewing his bone and flying one handed,
Barkstrong touched down, THE BEAGLE HAS LANDED!!!!

He climbs down the ladder and
takes a step back,
a small step for a dog, a giant
leap for the pack!

Barkstrong was the first dog on the moon,
Buzz joined him and played jumping all afternoon!

One last thing before the
team flies home,
Barkstrong digs a hole and
buries his bone!

So the boys fly the
moonship back up to Border,
then slingshot to Earth,
this was a tall order!

The team splashed down in the Pacific sea, Spacedog heroes they will always be!

THE END

Printed in Great Britain
by Amazon